Contents

Any words appearing in bold, **like this**, are explained in the Glossary

Introduction

We describe woodwind instruments as a single family, but in fact the term covers several different types of instrument. Each woodwind instrument produces sound in one of several different ways, and many are not made of wood at all – and never have been! This contrasts with, for example, brass instruments, which tend to be more similar in the way they produce sound, and the materials used to make them. This wide variety of designs means that woodwind instruments are used in all kinds of music throughout the world.

An orchestral woodwind section. Can you name any of the instruments?

Classical woodwind

The classical orchestra has a woodwind section which primarily consists of flutes, clarinets, oboes and bassoons, with some **compositions** calling for other, related instruments like the piccolo (a type of very small flute), the **bass** clarinet and contrabassoon (these are lower-**pitched** instruments).

Even in this one type of group, there are many differences in the instruments. For example, the modern concert flute is not usually made of wood, although the piccolo usually is, and in a beginners' orchestra (such as a school orchestra) many clarinetists use an instrument made of plastic rather than wood. The clarinet, oboe and bassoon are all **reed** instruments, but the clarinet has a **single reed**, whereas the oboe and bassoon have a **double reed**.

SOUNDBITES

Woodwind

Roger Thomas

Heinemann
LIBRARY

www.heinemann.co.uk/library
Visit our website to find out more information about Heinemann Library books.

To order:
☎ Phone 44 (0) 1865 888066
🗎 Send a fax to 44 (0) 1865 314091
💻 Visit the Heinemann Bookshop at www.heinemann.co.uk/library to browse our catalogue
and order online.

First published in Great Britain by Heinemann Library, Halley Court, Jordan Hill, Oxford, OX2 8EJ,
a division of Reed Educational and Professional Publishing Ltd.
Heinemann is a registered trademark of Reed Educational and Professional Publishing Ltd.

OXFORD MELBOURNE AUCKLAND
JOHANNESBURG BLANTYRE GABORONE
IBADAN PORTSMOUTH NH (USA) CHICAGO

Designed by Paul Davies and Associates
Originated by Ambassador Litho Ltd.
Printed at Wing King Tong in Hong Kong

ISBN 0 431 13071 X (hardback)   ISBN 0 431 13078 7 (paperback)
06 05 04 03 02   06 05 04 03 02
10 9 8 7 6 5 4 3 2   10 9 8 7 6 5 4 3 2 1

British Library Cataloguing in Publication Data

Thomas, Roger, 1956-
  Woodwind. - (Soundbites)
  1.Woodwind instruments - Juvenile literature 2.Woodwind
  instrument music - Juvenile literature
  I.Title
  788.2

Acknowledgements
The Publishers would like to thank the following for permission to reproduce photographs: Christian Him:
Pg.17; Corbis: Pg.24; Eyewire: Pg.7; Jazz Index/Christian Him: Pg.15, Pg.20, Pg.26, Pg.27, Pg.28; Lebrecht
Music Collection: Pg.4, Pg.7, Pg.9, Pg.14, Pg.18, Pg.19; Photodisc: Pg.8; Powerstock Zefa: Pg.23;
Redferns: Pg.5, Pg.11, Pg.13, Pg.22, Pg.25; Sally & Richard Greenhill: Pg.10; Trevor Clifford: Pg.6, Pg.12
(both), Pg.21; Yamaha: Pg.29.

Cover photograph reproduced with permission of Trevor Clifford and Photodisc.

Our thanks to John Ranck for his comments in the preparation of this book.

Every effort has been made to contact copyright holders of any material reproduced in this book.
Any omissions will be rectified in subsequent printings if notice is given to the publishers.

There are **concertos** (works for a soloist with an orchestra) and **sonatas** (for one instrument plus accompaniment, usually on a piano) written for most of these instruments. They are used in smaller groups (known as **chamber groups**) and in wind bands and **ensembles**, or as solo instruments.

Woodwind in jazz and rock

The saxophone, which began as a **military** band instrument, has had strong links with jazz for many years. However, the clarinet was the first important jazz woodwind instrument, and it is still widely used in many styles of jazz music. Many other woodwind instruments are used in jazz occasionally, including the flute, oboe and bassoon. Many rock bands can include a 'horn section', which will often include one or more saxophones, while others will include a single saxophone as a **melody** instrument.

Military and marching bands

Most types of **Western** woodwind instruments can be used in military and marching bands. Some, such as the saxophone and sarrusophone (a double-reed instrument) were originally designed for this purpose.

Folk and world music

Most musical cultures worldwide have their own specialized woodwind instruments. Some examples are discussed later in the book.

Woodwind instruments are an important part of jazz music.

How woodwind instruments work

Flutes and reeds

To play any woodwind instrument, the player blows into a **mouthpiece** to make the column of air inside the instrument vibrate. There are two main ways of making this happen, depending on the type of instrument. Some instruments have a sharp edge just inside the mouthpiece which splits the air into two, which causes the vibration.

The other main type of woodwind instrument has a thin, sharp piece of cane called a **reed**, which vibrates when the player blows against its edge, causing the column of air in the instrument to vibrate. The reed either vibrates against a mouthpiece (this is called a **single reed**) or another reed (a **double reed**), to which it is attached. On some reed instruments, such as the hornpipe (a historical folk instrument used in many parts of the world), the reed is a part of the tube which makes up the body of the instrument (this is called a fixed reed).

More notes

In all cultures, most woodwind instruments have something so that the player can change the notes played by the instrument. On some instruments, such as the recorder and flageolet (also called a 'tin whistle'), the player uses his or her fingers to cover a series of holes in the instrument to get the lowest note. By uncovering the different holes and allowing the air to escape, the player makes the column of vibrating air in the instrument shorter, which raises the **pitch** of the note. On some simple woodwind instruments, such as the swanee whistle and the bazana (a Nigerian flute used for 'talking' across distances), the player slides a plunger up and down the inside of the instrument to make the column of air shorter. Bazana players use one of their fingers as the plunger.

The clarinet is a reed instrument which has a key mechanism.

Modern **Western** woodwind instruments, such as the clarinet and saxophone, have a system of metal levers called **keys**, which are spring-loaded. Some have soft pads at one end. These pads cover the holes on the instrument until the key is pressed. This lifts up the pad and lets the air in. This system was invented because the holes in a woodwind instrument have to be in specific places so that the player can be sure that the instrument will play the correct notes, but on some instruments it is not possible to make the holes in positions which can be reached easily by the fingers. A system of keys allows the player to do this. Some instruments, such as the larger recorder, have a mixture of holes and keys. Some Chinese flutes have a piece of bamboo 'paper' stuck over one of the holes. This adds a buzz a bit like the noise of a **kazoo** to the sound.

The flageolet, or 'tin whistle', is widely used in Irish folk music.

A flute or not?

On some instruments, like South American panpipes (see page 23), the player blows across the top of the mouthpiece, with the opposite side of the mouthpiece providing the edge (this is what happens when you blow across the top of a bottle). However, because all these instruments work in the same way, **musicologists** will often classify them all as flutes.

The parts of a woodwind instrument

Reed instruments and flutes have some parts in common and some parts which are different. The examples shown here are the **alto** saxophone (a **single-reed** instrument) and the **descant** recorder (a type of flute), which are both very popular instruments. You will be able to identify the parts on most woodwind instruments using these two examples as a guide. The easiest way to see what the parts are for is to follow the path made by the player's breath as it travels from one end of the instrument to the other.

The parts of an alto saxophone

The REED (a) is a thin strip of cane which vibrates when the player blows against it. The saxophone is a single-reed instrument. The oboe and bassoon are both **double-reed** instruments. They have a 'sandwich' of two reeds tied together.

The **MOUTHPIECE** (b) is mainly used on single-reed instruments (although some early double-reed instruments also had a type of mouthpiece). It is hollow, and the reed is attached to it with a small clamp called the **ligature**. The gap between the reed and the mouthpiece is called the **lay**, which must be carefully set in order for the instrument to work properly (or at all!).

There are many parts on an alto saxophone!

8

The **CROOK** (c) is the top section of the hollow tube which makes up the body of the instrument. This can be removed to make it easier to clean the inside of the instrument and for packing the instrument away. The mouthpiece is pushed over a cork ring on the crook, which makes an airtight seal.

The **KEYS** (d) are attached to various springs and rods which will allow them to uncover or cover the correct holes on the instrument's body.

The PADS (e) for a saxophone are usually made of soft leather and cover the holes on the instrument. They are raised when the player presses the keys. The holes have a raised edge which 'bite' into the leather to give an airtight seal.

The **BELL** (f) is where the sound comes out. On some instruments, including most saxophones and the larger clarinets, the bell has a curved shape. On others, such as the **soprano** saxophone, the more popular higher-**pitched** clarinets and the bassoon, the bell is straight.

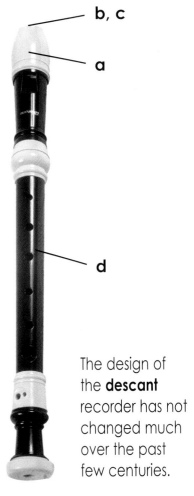

The parts of a descant recorder

The MOUTHPIECE (a) consists of a curved block. It can be detached for cleaning on some instruments.

The **WINDWAY** (b) is a slit in the mouthpiece through which the player blows.

The **LIP** (c) is a sharp edge which divides the player's breath, making the air in the instrument vibrate.

The HOLES (d) on the body of the instrument are covered and uncovered by the player's fingers to change the notes.

The design of the **descant** recorder has not changed much over the past few centuries.

Recorders and whistles

Recorders and whistles are among the most common types of woodwind instrument. Instruments which work in this way have a very long history and are found in many musical cultures throughout the world. These instruments all make a sound when air is blown over a sharp edge within the instrument's **mouthpiece**, which is joined to the body of the instrument in a straight line. **Musicologists** refer to these instruments as whistles to distinguish them from other instruments such as **side-blown flutes** (which include the modern orchestral flute). The term does not refer only to the sort of signalling whistles used by policemen and sports referees, although it does include them.

The recorder family

This group of instruments has remained virtually unchanged since the 16th century. Similar instruments have been found which date back 27,000 years. The name has nothing to do with sound recording but is taken from an old French word *'recordour'* which meant 'like birdsong'. The instrument has a gentle but lively sound which makes this a very appropriate name. The recorder was well-known in the 16th and 17th centuries, when they were often played by amateurs in groups (these groups were known as 'consorts'). Although the **transverse** side-blown flute became more popular than the recorder, for some time they were both used in classical music, such as in the famous 'Brandenburg Concertos' written by Johann Sebastian Bach (1685–1750).

Recorders are commonly one of the first instruments people will learn at school.

In 1919, the instrument maker Arnold Dolmetsch started a revival of interest in the instrument, and the subsequent development of inexpensive but accurate and hard-wearing plastic recorders made the instrument very popular for use in schools, as it is today.

There are several different sizes of recorder, of which the **descant** (known as the **soprano** in America) is the most popular. Other, larger sizes (in descending order of **pitch**) include the **treble** recorder, the **tenor** recorder and the **bass** recorder. The **sopranino** is smaller and higher in pitch than the descant. There is also a very small recorder called a '*kleine sopranino*', a German name which means 'little sopranino'(known as a piccolo recorder in America).

The penny whistle

The penny whistle is also known as the tin whistle, as it was once made of tin-plated steel (like tin cans). Today they are made in various sizes, often having a steel body and a hard plastic mouthpiece. This instrument is sometimes also referred to as the flageolet (see page 7). The penny whistle has a brighter, 'harder' **tone** than the recorder and is an important instrument in folk music, especially Irish folk music.

Andrea Corr, lead singer with the pop group The Corrs, uses the penny whistle in contemporary folk-rock.

Worldwide whistles

In other cultures, including those of India, Europe and South America, similar instruments are made from other materials, including wood, cane, clay and bone.

Side-blown/end-blown flutes

The **Western** concert flute commonly used in classical, jazz and band music is a **side-blown flute**. The sound is produced by blowing across the edge of the **mouthpiece**. This is like blowing across the top of a bottle, and some flutes, such as the Japanese shakuhachi, are played like this in a vertical position. These are called **end-blown flutes**. These flutes can sound similar to whistle flutes, but can be more 'breathy'. This is caused by air escaping across the top of the mouthpiece.

The Western flute family

The earliest ancestors of the Western concert flute were brought to Europe from the East in the 12th century. These early instruments had holes without **keys**. During the Middle Ages, the flute was mainly used in **military** music, but by the middle of the 17th century the flute had become accepted in orchestral music. Originally made of wood, the modern flute is now made of metal, but there are some exceptions.

A piccolo placed next to a standard concert flute shows the variety of sizes available.

Unusual flutes

The flute has been subjected to some rather strange ideas over the centuries. In the 1820s, an instrument maker named Laurent invented a flute made of glass. Complete with holes and keys, the instrument was a serious attempt to make a flute from an alternative material. There have also been porcelain flutes, flutes which are also walking sticks and a flute which concealed a dagger!

The piccolo (the smallest, highest-**pitched** flute) is generally made of wood because wooden instruments have a softer **tone**, although metal piccolos also exist, as do wooden instruments with metal mouthpieces. Also, flutes which are used to play earlier types of classical music, such as **Baroque** music, are often made of wood. These flutes are usually more simply made and have fewer keys.

The most usual type of concert flute is the second-highest in pitch. The piccolo plays higher notes, while the **alto** flute is lower in pitch and the **bass** flute lower still. The bass flute is easily recognized because of its shape, which is curved back on itself at the mouthpiece end, otherwise the instrument would be too long to play. One manufacturer has made a standard flute for children in the same style, so that they can play a full-sized instrument. The complicated system of keys on the flute was invented in the 1830s by a German player named Theobald Boehm. This system meant that the instrument would play in tune across its entire range. This had been a problem with earlier flutes. Boehm also established the idea of using metal, rather than wood, for the concert flute.

Worldwide flutes

Side-blown flutes remain central to Far Eastern music, where they are usually made of bamboo and come in many different sizes. Similar instruments are found in Africa, South America and Asia, where they originated in the 9th century.

The Japanese shakuhachi is an end-blown flute.

The clarinet family

The clarinet is a **single-reed** instrument (see page 6) and is widely used in classical music, traditional jazz and in **military** bands. Although single-reed instruments originated in ancient Egypt and similar instruments have existed in many cultures across the world since then, the first clarinets only came into use in about 1700. The oboe, bassoon and flute had already been used in European orchestras during the two centuries before this.

The clarinet was probably invented by a German maker named Johann Denner, who developed it from the chalumeau, a simpler single-reed instrument which had a body very like that of the recorder (see page 9). 'Clarinet' means 'little clarion'. The clarion was an early type of trumpet and the first clarinets were thought to have a similar sound. The modern clarinet has a 'liquid' **tone** which works especially well in bright, quick passages of music.

From left to right – the bass clarinet, b-flat and a clarinets.

Lots of clarinets

Today there is a wide range of clarinets in use, each covering a different range of notes. Orchestral players often have to change instruments during a single piece. In descending order of **pitch**, the instruments are referred to as the e-flat, b-flat and a clarinets (named after the keys in which they are designed to play), the **alto** clarinet, the basset horn (the name means 'little **bass** horn') and the bass clarinet. Because they play low notes, the alto clarinet and the basset horn have longer bodies, so these instruments have upturned **bells** at the bottom rather like an alto or **tenor** saxophone. There is also a very large **contrabass** clarinet, which is even lower than the bass clarinet. It has a big, curved body. It is not used often, but it can be played in some classical works such as Tchaikovsky's (1840–1893) 6th symphony. It is also sometimes used in **avant-garde** jazz by players such as Anthony Braxton.

Anthony Braxton is an avant-garde jazz player. Here he is playing the contrabass clarinet, a relatively unusual instrument.

What's it made of?

The type of wood used to make clarinets has changed over the centuries. Originally **boxwood** was used, but later two other woods, **ebony** and **grenadillo**, were used because they are harder. Some clarinets today, particularly student models, are made of a manufactured material called 'ebonite'. Metal is used for the key mechanism on all types of clarinet, but one manufacturer has produced a beginners' clarinet in which the whole instrument, including the **keys**, is made of plastic.

Across the world

There are a few examples of instruments in Africa and Asia which work in the same way as the clarinet, and a great many in South America. One interesting example is the tarogato, which was originally a **double-reed** instrument from Hungary. A single-reed version, looking like a clarinet with fewer keys and having a much harder tone, was invented by an instrument-maker named Schunda for use in one of Wagner's (1813–1883) operas. It has since been used by some avant-garde musicians.

The saxophone family

Saxophones are similar to clarinets in terms of how the instruments work. Both have a single **reed** and a system of **keys** and pads. However, the saxophone is also similar to the oboe, in that the tube is shaped like a narrow cone, while the clarinet is really a straight tube which has a flared **bell** at the end. Although usually made of brass, the saxophone is classed as a woodwind instrument because its sound is produced by a reed rather than with a lip pressure on a cup-shaped **mouthpiece**, as with true brass instruments. It is used extensively in jazz, in wind bands and marching bands, in rock and pop and also in some 20th century classical music. The saxophone generally has a brighter, harder **tone** than the clarinet.

Adolphe Sax and his big family

Adolphe Sax was a Belgian instrument maker who worked in Paris. He invented the saxophone in around 1840 as a family of instruments for use in military bands. Originally available in fourteen different sizes, the four most popular sizes available today are, in descending order of **pitch**, the **soprano**, the **alto**, the **tenor** and the **baritone**. These four sizes can be played together in a saxophone **quartet**, playing both classical and jazz-derived music. The **sopranino**, which is higher-pitched than the soprano, is also used, although it is less popular, as is the **bass** saxophone. The **contrabass** (lower than the bass) also exists, but experts believe there are only about fifteen working contrabasses in use today worldwide. The 'C-**melody**' saxophone was originally created for beginners and amateurs, as it was designed to play the melody part of music written for the piano. Examples are hard to find today, but are often sought out by specialists.

The expressive 'sax'

Despite its origins, the saxophone became the single most significant instrument in jazz, because variations in playing technique allowed saxophonists to develop their own individual sounds on the instrument. Some of the many important saxophonists are Coleman Hawkins (1904–1969), who first popularized the saxophone's expressive capabilities, Charlie Parker (1920–55), who explored a highly complex style on the instrument, John Coltrane (1926–67), who developed a unique approach to extended improvised **solos** and Michael Brecker (born 1949) whose **contemporary** style has infuenced many younger players.

Classical, pop and rock music

The alto has traditionally been the most widely-used saxophone in classical music. More recently, other types of saxophone, such as the

The tenor is one of the most widely-played saxophones, especially in jazz.

soprano, have become more prominent in classical **composition**. Early forms of American popular music, such as R & B ('rhythm and blues'), country blues and swing, were all influenced by jazz elements. What is usually regarded as the first rock'n'roll recording, 'Rocket 88' by The Kings of Rhythm, featured the saxophone. Today, many rock bands include a saxophonist, either as a soloist or as part of a horn section.

Double-reed instruments

Double-reed instruments have two **reeds** which are bound tightly together. When the player blows through the instrument, air is forced between the reeds, making them vibrate. One of the earliest double-reed instruments was an ancient Greek instrument called the aulos, some examples of which date back to around 2800 BCE. It looked a little bit like a recorder (see page 9) but had a double reed inside it. The aulos needed a huge amount of wind pressure in order to work properly, which meant that players would often wear straps around their faces to make their cheeks stronger!

The modern oboe family, shown in descending order of pitch.

Some early double-reeds and the first oboes

The oboe is said to have been invented in France by the instrument maker and musician Jean Hotteterre in the mid-1600s. It was probably developed from an earlier instrument, the **treble** shawm, which was very loud and best suited to playing outdoors. The oboe was designed to be a quieter instrument, suitable for playing indoors. During the **Renaissance**, many other double-reed instruments were in use. These included the courtaut, made from a single piece of wood but containing two wind channels, the crumhorn, a hook-shaped instrument with a distinctive **tone** and the wonderfully-named racket, which was shaped like a bottle with a mouthpiece attached, and had a very long tube inside it, folded into a zig-zag shape.

The modern oboe family

The modern oboe is made of wood and has a system of **keys** which work in a similar way to those of the flute, clarinet and saxophone (see pages 12–17). There are four sizes in general use. The oboe as such is the highest in **pitch** and the most widely used. The oboe d'amore is slightly larger and lower in pitch. However, in about 1770, it fell out of use, until the fashion for using authentic instruments for performing early classical music revived interest in the instrument over 100 years later. The cor Anglais (also known in translation as 'the English horn', despite having been invented in Italy and not being a horn) is still lower in pitch, while the **baritone** oboe is lower still. Music written for the baritone oboe is often played on a similar German instrument called a heckelphone.

The bassoon

The bassoon was developed in the late 17th century from a similar earlier instrument called the curtal. The bassoon has a doubled-back wooden tube with keys and is played through a **crook**. As the name implies, the bassoon is a **bass** instrument, but there is also a contrabassoon which is lower still. Its tube is over six metres long and is folded into four.

The contrabassoon has the lowest pitch of all the oboe family.

Music for double-reeds

The oboe and bassoon families are mainly played in classical, general orchestral and wind band music. They are also very occasionally used by jazz players. Shawm-like double-reed instruments, such as a Turkish instrument called the zurna, are widely used in other musical cultures.

Some very unusual woodwind instruments

Within the different instrumental families discussed in this book so far, there are many instruments which are less common than others. These include instruments which can play extremely high or low notes (such as the **sopranino** saxophone and the **contrabass** clarinet), historical instruments which have no real equivalent today, but which have been rediscovered or reconstructed by instrument makers (such as the aulos and the racket) and instruments which have been adopted into **Western** music from other cultures (such as the tarogato).

The distinctive baritone saxophone can play lower notes than the more usual alto and tenor saxophones.

Some unusual instruments may never have become popular. Some examples will have been invented for a specific piece of music. Some may have been devised by individual musicians looking for a new sound or other benefits. Here are a few examples.

How low can you get?

Adolphe Sax (see pages 16 and 17) had made plans for **subcontrabass** instruments (subcontrabass is even lower than contrabass), and various **prototypes** were shown at trade fairs and exhibitions. However, producing useful notes of such low **pitch** on a woodwind instrument was next to impossible, and the inventor was often ridiculed for his attempts.

The saxello

During the 1920s, many instrument makers experimented with new saxophone shapes. The saxello, made by an American company, was basically a **soprano** saxophone with a 45 degree curve at the top and a 90 degree outward curve at the bottom. Some examples survive today, and the British saxophonist Elton Dean plays one regularly.

The manzello and the stritch

The jazz saxophonist Rahsaan Roland Kirk (1936–1977) had many innovative ideas. He would often play two or three instruments simultaneously, and he also modified a saxello and an **alto** saxophone with extra **keys** and re-shaped **bells**. He called these unique customized instruments the 'manzello' and the 'stritch'.

The saxello is an elegant re-design of the soprano saxophone. Today, it is quite a rare instrument.

The sarrusophone

The quiet tones of the oboe and bassoon were not ideal for use in **military** bands, so in 1856, a bandmaster named Sarrus designed a group of eight **double-reed** band instruments with brass bodies, which varied in shape according to the size of the instrument – for example, the soprano sarrusophone was a small, straight instrument which looked like a brass oboe, whereas the much larger contrabass looked a bit like a tuba. However, all the instruments had keys and pads like conventional woodwind instruments, and as with the saxophone, the sarrusophone is a member of the woodwind family because it is a **reed** instrument, despite being made of brass. Few examples are in use today, but the woodwind player Gerald Oshita has made recordings using the contrabass sarrusophone, in which he uses its distinctive 'burping' **tone** very effectively!

Non-Western and folk woodwind instruments

Many of the instruments in this book are of non-**Western** origin, while others are mainly associated with folk music, but there are far more woodwind instruments that have remained unique to their specific cultures. However, the increased Western interest in 'world music' has meant that we are far more likely to hear the music made by these instruments, either in performance or as recordings, than at any other time in world history. Here are two examples.

Bagpipes

This family of instruments has been known since Roman times, and can be found in Asia, North Africa and Europe. Their sound comes from **single**- or **double**-**reeds**, the notes are changed by covering holes with the fingers and the air which causes the **reeds** to vibrate comes from the player's breath – any resemblance to other woodwind instruments ends there!

Bagpipes work by having a large bag, usually made of animal skin (sometimes covered with decorative fabric), which the player must keep inflated by blowing into a tube. When the bag is full, the player begins squeezing the air out through one or several tubes which contain reeds, while at the same time

You can recognize the distinctive sound of bagpipes anywhere!

blowing more air into the bag. This means that the player can pause to take a breath without having to stop playing. On some smaller pipes, such as the Irish uilleann pipes, the air comes from bellows squeezed under the player's arm, hence the name – 'uilleann' means 'elbow'. The main pipe, which has holes for changing the notes, is called the **chanter**. The other pipes, each of which play an accompanying single note, are called **drones**. Bagpipes are usually associated with traditional music written specifically for them, but one musician named Rufus Harley uses them as a jazz instrument, with very unusual results.

The panpipes or syrinx

The panpipes, or syrinx, consist of a set of single-note **end-blown flutes** (see page 12) fixed together in a line. They are played by blowing across the tops of the tubes. Traditionally made of cane, wood, clay or stone, there are also modern versions, including toy versions, made from metal or plastic. They have been used for over 2000 years, and are still played in South America, Europe, and Japan, to name but a few countries. Because the notes played by each pipe cannot be changed, a group of players will often have instruments which play different sets of notes. They will then 'take turns' to play the notes needed for a **melody**. Like the bagpipes, the panpipes are usually played in traditional **indigenous** music, but Mozart used some toy panpipes as a sound effect in his opera 'The Magic Flute'.

Panpipes have been used for over 2000 years. This South American musician is playing a modern version of the instrument.

23

Woodwind players in jazz, rock and pop

Like most other instruments, woodwinds became adopted into jazz and popular forms of music, rather than being made for them. This has led to a number of different woodwind instruments being used in many different ways in these areas of music.

It is now quite usual for a jazz musician to specialize in playing different woodwind instruments like the clarinet.

Woodwinds in jazz

Jazz is a very diverse form of music, and the saxophone, clarinet and other woodwind instruments are used in many different contexts, including small groups, big bands and even in unaccompanied **solo** performances. The techniques required for playing various woodwind instruments tend to overlap, which means that it is quite usual for a jazz musician to have a main instrument and to double on a second, or to specialize in unusual instruments, or even, in a few cases, to play the whole range of woodwind instruments.

Small group jazz may involve a 'rhythm section' (piano, bass and drums) with a single saxophonist playing the main **melody**. In traditional jazz, this role is often taken by the clarinet. However, many musicians have demonstrated that other woodwind instruments can be used very effectively in jazz. The next page gives you a few examples.

- The American Bob Cooper (1925–93) and the British Karl Jenkins (born 1944) have both used the oboe in jazz.
- The American Illinois Jacquet (born 1922) and the British Lindsay Cooper have both played the bassoon in jazz bands.
- The American Herbie Mann (born 1930) the British Bob Downes (born 1937) both play the saxophone but are more noted for specializing in the flute. Downes has also made extensive use of non-Western bamboo flutes. The American James Newton (born 1953) has devoted himself entirely to the flute, using many advanced techniques.
- The American Eric Dolphy (1928–64) played **alto** saxophone, flute and **bass** clarinet.

Woodwinds in rock and pop

This type of musical style tends to go in and out of fashion. A saxophone can be added to a rock band to add an alternative melodic 'voice' to the usual line up of lead guitar, keyboards and vocals. A few rock bands made the atmospheric sound of the flute into a musical trademark, while a few other players have adventurously added other woodwinds.

A rock and pop 'horn section' is a small group of wind instrumentalists used to add backing to a rock band. It will usually include one or more saxophones alongside brass instruments.

The British band Jethro Tull featured the band's leader, Ian Anderson, on flute. As these fragile instruments would often become damaged, Anderson kept several spares onstage – in a bucket!

Woodwind recording and performance technology

Woodwind instruments have several important roles within **contemporary** rock and pop music, and this is reflected in the way in which this family of instruments is used on stage and in the production of recordings. Also, the nature of jazz, rock and pop performances has changed enormously, with audiences having very high expectations. All of these problems are dealt with by modern electronic and **acoustic** technology, and it is important for modern woodwind players who work in these areas to have at least some understanding of these subjects.

Woodwind onstage

There are many situations in which woodwind instruments will need to be **amplified** for use onstage. This may apply to a jazz **soloist** playing to a large audience, to a horn section backing a rock band, or to a light orchestra or **big band**. In each case, there are two main ways of amplifying woodwind instruments.

One method of amplifying woodwind instruments is to use a microphone on a stand.

One or more microphones can be set up in front of the player, or a microphone can be physically attached to the instrument. The signals from the microphone are then fed to a **mixer**, which is used to balance the sound with the sound of the other instruments and voices onstage. The mixture of signals then passes to an **amplifier** and loudspeakers, which relay the overall sound to the audience or listener.

Woodwind and microphones

There are advantages and disadvantages to both kinds of microphone. A microphone standing in front of the player allows more direct control of the instrument's sound.

Another method is to attach the microphone to the instrument itself.

Sometimes two or more saxophonists can share a single microphone, which allows the sounds of their instruments to blend naturally before they reach the mixer.

A microphone attached directly to the instrument is more suited to players who are playing continuously. It allows the player to move around the stage, just as guitarists and vocalists do. It also allows the sound of the instrument to be easily processed through electronic effects such as **echo**, which the player can control onstage with foot pedals. However, because the position of the instrument in relation to the microphone cannot be changed during a performance, all changes in the instrument's sound – even simple ones, such as volume – have to be controlled electronically, either by the performer or by the sound engineer.

27

Innovative woodwinds

The woodwind family is thousands of years old, yet the fundamental way in which this type of instrument works – air produced by the player's breath vibrating in a tube – has remained constant throughout this time. However, the materials of which the instruments are actually made has constantly evolved, and **digital** technology has now added a totally new dimension.

The plastic Grafton saxophone was invented because of the shortage of metal during World War II.

Where's the wood?

Throughout the centuries, instrument makers have varied and developed the materials they use to make woodwind instruments, in order to improve or change the sounds they make. Examples referred to in this book include clay, bone, metal and plastic. Some of these innovations, such as ebonite (see page 15) have remained in use.

Elegant plastics

One of the most celebrated examples of new materials used for woodwind instruments was the 'Grafton Acrylic' **alto** saxophone. This was devised by the Italian inventor Ettore Sommaruga in the early 1940s. Metal was in short supply because of World War II, so Sommaruga designed an instrument with a body made of a hard plastic called acrylic. Metal was only used for the **crook** and the **keys**. The famous saxophonist Charlie Parker was often short of money, and would sometimes need to **pawn** his usual instrument, keeping a Grafton as a spare. Another respected saxophonist, Ornette Coleman, bought one every year until they ceased to be available. These instruments are prized collectors' items today.

Cool colours

Another innovation was the use of coloured or tinted **lacquers** on saxophones. This began fairly late on in the history of the instrument, but black, white, red and other coloured saxophones can be found quite easily today.

Digital days

Initially, the electronic modification of woodwinds was restricted to processing the sounds made by existing instruments (see page 26 and 27). This was to change with the invention of a computer language called **MIDI** (musical instrument digital interface) which allows digital data to be transmitted from one electronic musical instrument to others. This would, for example, allow one electronic keyboard instrument to access and play the sounds of another. The idea was later extended to woodwind-type instruments. These worked by using electronic sensors to 'translate' the pressure of the player's breath and fingers into data. This would then trigger the required sounds from a **digital sound module**, where sounds could be created and stored. This effectively allowed the player to choose the sound of any instrument – or non-instrument – at all. The data produced can also be stored digitally for playback or editing at a later stage. Several major manufacturers, including Yamaha and Casio, have produced such instruments. While they look unconventional, they have recognizable **keys** and **mouthpieces**. The development of the woodwind family is clearly not over yet!

Digital woodwinds, like this Yamaha WX5 are the latest generation of a very old instrumental family.

Glossary

acoustic referring to sound; also means unamplified

alto a pitch range which is lower than soprano but higher than tenor

amplifier an electronic device which makes sound louder

avant-garde modern and experimental

Baroque a cultural period in Europe in the 17th and 18th centuries

bass the lowest range of notes in normal use (contrabass and subcontrabass are lower still)

bell the flared end of an instrument through which the sound emerges

big band a jazz orchestra

boxwood the wood of the box tree; used for making some woodwind instruments

chamber groups small ensembles which play classical music

chanter a pipe used on bagpipes which produces the melody

composition a piece of written music

concertos works written for an orchestra plus (usually) a single instrumental soloist

contemporary of the present day

contrabass a pitch range which is lower than bass

crook the curved end of a wind instrument

descant a term sometimes used as the equivalent of soprano

digital using a computer-type 'language' of electronic ones and zeros

digital sound module a digital device which contains a stored memory of sounds

double reed two reeds bound together

drones pipes on bagpipes which produce a fixed note

ebony a type of very hard, black wood which is used to make some woodwind instruments

echo a repeat of a sound caused by the noise reflecting back to the listener

end-blown flute a type of flute which is played vertically

ensembles small classical music groups

flageolet refers to both an older type of woodwind instrument and to the Irish 'penny whistle'

grenadillo a type of wood used for making woodwind instruments

indigenous native to a particular place

kazoo an instrument which changes the voice with a vibrating diaphragm when the player hums or sings into it

keys finger-operated levers which open and close the holes on a wind instrument

lacquer varnish

lay the gap between the reed and the mouthpiece on a reed instrument

ligature a clip which attaches the reed to the mouthpiece of a clarinet or saxophone

lip sharp edge in the mouthpiece which divides the player's breath

melody the main tune in a piece of music

MIDI stands for musical instrument digital interface; a type of computer language which allows some electronic instruments to exchange data with computers or each other

military to do with the armed forces

mixer an electronic device which blends the sounds from several microphones or electronic instruments

mouthpiece part of the instrument through which the player blows

musicologists people who study aspects of music other than performance or composition, such as the history of the subject

pawn to leave an object with a pawnbroker in return for money lent – if the money is not paid back then the pawnbroker can sell the object to make up the money

pitch how high or low a note is

prototype an initial, experimental version of a final product

quartet a group consisting of four musicians

reed a strip of cane which vibrates when air is blown across it

Renaissance the artistic and cultural revival in Europe during the 14th, 15th and 16th centuries

side-blown flute a flute which is played by blowing sideways across the mouthpiece

single reed a type of instrument which has a single reed fixed against a mouthpiece, as opposed to a double reed, which has two reeds bound together

solo/ist a section of music or a composition which features a single musician, or which is played by one musician alone; a musician playing such music

sonatas compositions for a single instrument, generally with a keyboard accompaniment (although keyboard sonatas are solo works)

sopranino a pitch range higher than soprano

soprano a pitch range higher than alto but lower than sopranino – the highest range in general use

subcontrabass the lowest pitch range

tenor a pitch range lower than alto but higher than baritone

tone The quality of a sound – often referred to in terms of colour or shade – dark, bright etc.

transverse across

treble refers to a high pitch range

windway the part of a recorder which allows the air to pass from the mouthpiece into the instrument

West/ern used by musicologists to refer to the music of Europe and the English speaking world

INDEX